CONFIDENCE IN CONTROL

CONFIDENCE IN CONTROL

LUNA EMBER

CONTENTS

CHAPTER 1

Introduction

Becoming a dominant woman in a relationship can give a sense of comfort and self-esteem. It can make ugly things beautiful, dissolve differences, and petty frustrations. Often, a dominant woman is closer to being a person who is difficult to anger, hard to provoke, and hardly ever visibly impressed by a guy - without being bitchy, arrogant, or hypocritical. Instead, she is playful, humorous, unique, or quirky and not afraid to stand up for her rights or be equally independent and self-reliant. In the long run, this even task distribution will bear the most satisfying, long-lasting rewards for both partners involved. Her apparent self-esteem may draw him to her with an irresistible intensity, taking further what was only a vague affinity to dominance and control. There is a right time and a right place for everything we have in mind, and you are the one allowed to make these tough decisions for both of you.

A girl's girlfriend taunts her for letting the boyfriend order her about and tie her to the bedposts with her own silk scarves. But she forgets all the intimidating looks some female quest participants are giving her and thinks hard. Should she accept this vicarious dominance, appointed by someone who has forgotten how amusing it once was to pretend a man is an imperial Chinese emperor, coolly ordering you even in sleep? Discussing relationships with her peers would truly be the highest art if such dialogues could be interestedly followed by recorded playbacks of the night. Not everyone can offer a vast palace, a large harem, handsome eunuchs, intricate baths, and wall-to-wall carpet richly loomed into static patterns shown in meticulously inlaid marble floors. And they care if you're enjoying the co-creation of elaborate storylines from best-selling books and heightened attention to intricate detailing, exploring uncharted depths from provocative slumbers into foxy waking delights. Enjoy them too; relish this dominating yet playful relationship.

Purpose of the Guide

The illustrated guide was written for women who want to take a more dominant role in their romantic relationships. A theme worth remembering as you read this book - people who care for and respect their partners are too valuable to be abusive. Real love and respect are the basis for any successful relationship. The guide is written in detail because the author feels that understanding the reasons for the suggestions and actions is helpful, and because this book is for beginners. The step-by-step instructions should make it easier for the beginner to take the first steps into the world of dominance.

The new dominant might have friends who are already doms, and will undoubtedly be exposed to these people and their ideas. This guide is written to help those women who might want to become doms by themselves, and does not explain the ideas or philosophy of the BDSM world. Terminology will be explained in the glossary at the end of the guide. While she is fairly well-versed in the world of BDSM, an author is heterosexually-oriented and the examples might seem quite heterosexually oriented. Please try to adapt the suggestions to fit your own romantic relationships. With a willing partner, the suggestions can work just as easily in a homosexual relationship.

CHAPTER 2

Understanding Female Sexual Dominance

Female sexual dominance is the practice of consensual dominance and submission, which may be rooted in childhood fantasy play and spankings. It is not about overt violence, gangsterism, or anger. Female sexual dominance is a consensual form of sexuality involving a specific form of mutually pleasurable and consensual intimate personal power exchange. Important features in such a relationship are that safewords are established and agreed upon in advance, and that a climate of mutual responsibility exists. Emphasize the essence of power as a unique form of trust. Trust is said to be the essence of power. The relinquishing of control is as essential an act as the wielding of control. A safe, sane, consensual environment is inherent in this depiction.

The concept of power in the context of sexuality and trust is as complex as it is fascinating. The essence of any woman's power comes from her person, her body, herself. Power through self-empowerment leads to her personal possession of her own power. Power through the esteem and admiration of others is reliant on mutual respect, mutual affection. In this idealized context, the possessive, coercive, or jealous behavior of one person who professes love for another is not love at all, but rather a form of violence. Such a far-from-powerful individual is actually far from power.

Definition and Concepts

Sexual power - arousing the desire of or controlling the sexual activities of another. Female power - possessing traits which are traditionally characteristic of males in a particular society or community. Clearly, control or authority concerning sex, in a society where men dominate, is power in itself. Woman as sexually controlling is therefore a powerful and dangerous force, consciousness of which may also be a cause of the precariousness of male confidence. The eroticization of power can give confidence - if you are powerful in sex, you are powerful. This kind of power has no limit - unlike other sources of power, it is never exhausted. Because it is a source of empowerment and transgression, female sexual control is dependent upon and reinforcing of societal, social, moral and societal representations of sexual difference. It offers a challenge to these conventional differences and relations of power. Whether the nature of female sexual control is understood as antithetical or transgressive with respect to conventional gender representations and male/female relationships of domination - it is different.

The repetition of these differentiations produces a transforming power. Power relations are a network of domination which saturate the whole social and sexual body right down to its smallest cell. The counterpointed nature of female control appears is not in dispute - it functions as an established procedure for the possessor of vital power. The principal motive for the exercise of female control is the pleasure which it procures for the mother, rather than for the child. Amongst conventional sexual contacts, rather than one-sided predominance, woman has become the controlling, dominant force. Control and affirmation are the goads which force a chastising morality to express its true nature. A woman who controls shows that she exists as an autonomous individual. We know the status of woman because the law tells us, she has power only when she knows what she wants.

Historical and Cultural Perspectives

In an era when women are gaining equal access to controls in the boardroom, increasingly exemplifying instrumental and active sexual agency is an important initiative. Jenny Holzer very famously wrote "You have no idea what a poor opinion I have of myself, and how little I enjoy spending time with you," and sometimes I feel like she is speaking directly for the female sex. A lot of the outside world, our media, our art, our erotic imagery, is full of examples of women submitting or being subjugated. Our sexual energy has leaked. We were the receivers. Women have been the object of sexual dis-irony for so long that in today's atmosphere of faux progressiveness, many people pay more attention to a boobs metaphor than to a strong woman.

Meaning Western culture is not the only representation we meet with. Many societies have some tradition of a male-dominated household. The English word "husband" comes from the Old Norse word "husbondi" translating to "master of the house." At the very beginning of The Female Woman, Betty Friedan responds to the idea of a traditional feminine role with "but not all girls want to be a girl." There are many parallel reactions to outmoded ideas of what it means to be female. Some people base their femininity on the belief that they can rightly and responsibly control their existence. They find self-worth in this agency and sexual gratification. At the end of a working day, so long and full of compromises, a woman looks in the mirror and asks herself: Am I a girl? Can she be hard and soft at the same time? Can I actively participate in the basic instinct at the heart of all other issues and obstinate proofs of sterility? The answer that this book provides is YES.

6 – LUNA EMBER

heart of all other issues and obstinate proofs of sterility? The answer that this book provides is YES.

CHAPTER 3

Benefits and Challenges of Female Sexual Dominance

"'Dominance' brings to mind adjectives such as 'tough,' 'tough as nails' for women, but when we choke or bitch-manage, we don't want partners who cry alone at home." Some people want partners who cry alone at home, but when this want is a scene developed for sex with a partner, as described in strength as part of a sex act in partners. Then, conceptually, this difference in application is readily apparent and recognizable, desirable component of strong, when we talk about looks." So, what is sexual dominance composed of, if not toughness or being tough as nails? Clearly, it is made up of other, deeply-felt, other-regarding, caring qualities. Care and feeding, ministrations, nurturance, being bossy bossy, strength, stewardship, sensitivity, understanding when you want and don't feel strong, staying in touch, kind but strong and bossy, and quiet strength - strength in silence. And based on these qualities, the benefits of sexual dominance are truly valuable.

A woman in a satisfying sexual dominance relationship with a man derived several benefits. She felt she received a level of trust from him that few people ever received. She understood not only him, but many men better now because of her experience. She enjoyed being bossy, and received satisfaction and pleasure from being the boss. There were a great many opportunities for her to learn during sexual dominance activities - she had learned a lot about herself. After experiencing sexual dominance, she felt she could be more assured and confident about herself as a woman. She enjoyed the power women could hold over men. The feeling of awe she experienced at the depths of femininity which the man reached reinforced her own sense of femininity. The pride in the enjoyment she had given her partner was an experience, independent of the level of the role, in that her partner should be seen proud of her for what she had done to and for him. Additionally with her partner, there was felt an intimate bond. She understood him, and he appreciated her. She had allowed another man to give himself to her, and learned that this in and of itself may be a gift, warranting a hard choice to be made in thanking him. Then, also, she had learned what some men really wanted from their women and how to give that to them.

Empowerment and Self-Expression
Empowerment, a phrase much in currency today, is used to invoke self-awareness, autonomy, independence, and vigorous capability. It is the quality from which self-confidence springs, characterizing the state of being strong, secure, and set in one's conscious abilities. In the case of women seeking the fulfillment of sexual control desires, it is the necessary underpinning to any kind of self-imposed discipline and control. Once taken in hand, it also releases other qualities that provide useful in other parts of one's life, when handling boundaries and decisions.

Having a lack of confidence, self-esteem, poise, and comfort with one's sexuality, seeking empowerment becomes almost a duty, for confidence is what supports other forms of self-control. Such as sexual control and discipline, which can lead to sexual grace and pleasure, as well as self-expression, proper initiation, and programmatic exploration of the darklands which can be encountered during the implementation of one's desires. Since satisfying desires is a quest for a state of satisfaction, self-expression is the successful conveyance of personal feelings. Recognizing that the self-respecting way to seek fulfillment is to serve and bring joy to another, however, is an effort that grows continuously stronger with time, particularly as the reactive partner stimulates your emergence as a being responsive to the needs and desires of another.

Navigating Stereotypes and Misconceptions
The woman is said to be the power behind the man, but for the man, power comes from accepting the role of leader. As in daily life, the daily ceremonial transfer of power is fraught with difficulty. To start with, not surprisingly, there is a particular kind of man who likes to go submissive and a particular kind of woman who likes to take charge. And then, once it becomes public knowledge, the man at least faces a disconcerting range of potential sniggers due to imported stereotypes and misconceptions. Does it necessarily signify a lack of masculinity, the modern version of the ancient proverbial rib or carpet, or the petticoat government that the name suggested in a bygone age? Taken to its logical conclusion, does it lie somewhere between schoolboyish role-play and indirect homosexuality or even full-blown transvestism? Or possibly heavy frigidity?

CHAPTER 4

Building Confidence as a Female Dominant

What are the secrets of successful female dominants? More than a few are displayed in this book: smile, savor your partner's reactions and feelings, avoid taking things too seriously, maintain humor, and practice naturalness and honesty. Other successful dominants might add: don't strive for perfection or power; see the authority to which others defer not as power, but as responsibility; and build your confidence by concentrating on how your dominance will enhance your life and self-awareness. Domination of another is an intimacy, but no matter how deep that element of your relationship, it is also play. Though your dominance may be spiritually significant and meaningful, and potentially alter the relationship, feel free to exercise play with your partner, to be amused at your hidden powers and his hidden reactions.

In our experiences and travels, we've talked with people who enjoy female sexual dominance, and observed them in both casual and intimate settings. A plethora of successful methods and attitudes are used for achieving female dominance. About building confidence states that you take command of yourself and have faith that the world will accept you. Clearly that is, to a degree, the essence of any confidence - personal, professional, philosophical, religious, or sexual. What special unique characteristics, rules, and techniques do female dominants convey? In other words, how is female dominance different from any other kind of confidence, for individuals who are blessed with it? What are covert methods that a woman might use towards cultivating confidence in her female power and sexuality? Let's look at what female dominants say about themselves - through the messages they send us.

Self-Exploration and Awareness

Self-exploration and self-awareness help to prepare women for their role of leadership within relationships. If we are to feel confident and self-assured, we must first confirm to ourselves that we are worthy of that belief. When we challenge a male to see our strength, it is necessary that we have the strength; when we ask for his respect, it is essential that we also have self-respect. Despite the knowledge that on many levels we wish to adopt an unequal role for our relationships, our acceptance starts from the understanding that we, as a person, are not unequal. That whatever assumptions may have to be drawn from our choice of a dominant lifestyle, they do not apply to our general sense of self-worth, intelligence, or physical presence. We are strong individuals in the full sense of the word, and should never embrace a role that depends on any less strength for its validity. In many ways, in order to accept a higher standing within our relationship, we have to first accept a higher standing within ourselves. Once you truly believe in your own strength, intelligence and pride, it will be extremely difficult to accept the 'traditional view'. As a dominant woman, those perceptions are seldom embraced by those around us. Yet, on the inside we may feel obligated to take on the submissive role. And we may be deeply troubled by the internal conflict that results. Questions arise: Am I living a lie? Who engages in the most inappropriate or irrational behavior? The individual who is strong, creative, confident, free, and happy or the individual who is confined to traditional sex roles? Who can be classified as the most normal? The pattern becomes obvious. Our development as children and adolescents (both male and female) quenched our spirit of individuality and independence and made us conform to a pattern of development that has produced adults who cannot think or act for themselves. Opportunities for self-growth are limited, and our doubts and fears lead to interpersonal and intrapsychic conflicts. They can also put us into a particularly vulnerable and dependent position that is difficult to escape.

Having determined that male authority is not always the most sound, it then becomes necessary to determine what qualities we want or can accept in the male we wish to lead. There are countless traits that, in one woman's way, make the male an attractive potential submissive. Which traits or abilities are important to each of us?

What are the rewards of that special, unique relationship between those who are traditionally strangers in the world? A man to be the most incredible, special of men. A woman to be the most incredible and special of women. Indeed, the male to play the supportive and caring role, rather than seek his inspiration from the aging god, Apollo. The playmate, the virgin; the red rose; the Queen; the dominant female; the erotic suppress. Both must develop self-awareness in order to make this kind of exchange possible and to believe in the worth that others may see hidden within them. In the long run, no society should exist that ignores the vital problem of encouraging its women to demand every potential for living full, rewarding lives at the same time that the individual is encouraged to accept such attributes as physical strength, clear thinking, and intelligence, self-confidence, protecting maternal instincts, and a strong desire to be cared for. This is a means by which society can encourage those traits in its members, district physical health and well-being, and the personal strength needed to meet the multifaceted responsibilities of modern living. It is in the interest of society at large to prevent antiquated sex-role-stereotyping from becoming the sole criterion for measuring personal fulfillment.

Communication and Boundaries

While it is important to maintain the upper hand in a BDSM scene, it does not mean that there should be any miscommunication between you and your partner. Communication is one of the keys to any successful relationship—particularly a D/s one. The stronger the relationship you develop with your partner, the more that you each will share in the experiences you undertake together. BDSM is about growth and exploration. Be ready to learn new things about yourself and your partner, and to strive to keep that line of communication open. It's no longer enough to say, "You should have communicated that you needed more of X." If you need something, say so. It's incumbent on the submissive to speak up, you say? So be it. I'm telling you: speak up. Ask for what you need.

Part of this communication is the distinct drawing of boundaries—specifically, the point at which a boundary can be safely crossed. It is your responsibility to create a mental picture of where the edge is. You are basically saying, "Within these bounds we will play together, and you do not have to worry about overstepping a serious line." It is then your partner's responsibility to respect these boundaries. The worst violation a voyeur can commit is moving without permission. That kind of violation can be lethal. Establish boundaries between scenes as well. Does your relationship allow you to check in after a scene? If so, how? etc.

CHAPTER 5

Exploring Different Forms of Female Dominance

What would be the point of discovering that we had a nationality and not of discovering also that others had one too? When one travels, it is because it is a habit to move. When I meet others who are looking still for their habit, perhaps for an impossible journey, perhaps for the desert, why, then I can weigh anchor and be on the move all at once without leaving the room. We had seen an appetite for notice, one that was getting fierce and that no application to any other authority satisfied. In the absence of an obvious target, it turned to its prisons, which absorbed it still further. The epochs of our lives are bound by the sentences of local people who killed the sentence and the sentence that killed them italicizes them in act in our stupid capitals. The local people are convinced their sentence is the one that counted most.

One of the most intriguing things about female dominance to me is the number of different forms it takes. I know many different women in various successful D/s relationships and they run the gamut in terms of personality, style, and the symbolic aspects. Yet they are all clearly dominant. By exploring the diversity in this lifestyle, I hope to add to the universal literature on the relationship that is the emotional heart of the dominant lifestyle. These personal stories may help other women who are seeking to develop a clearer self-awareness of their dominant features, their longing for deeper and more intimate, open relationships, and who feel more capable of finding this through careful, balanced dominance. And by providing models, lessen feelings of alienation among those who struggle. I have taken up the sword of writing and political action in my effort to do something along these lines for all of us who are looking for women-friendly, nonbondage or pain-related books, conferences, and stories to enjoy. Just atop this essay, following my summing-up, is a list of the areas I will be covering here.

Physical Domination

A lot of people seem to think that if you are dominant or controlling, that this means that you have to be dominant or controlling all the time. Worse yet, they seem to think that being in control means acting like a dominatrix. After all, isn't sexual dominance all about dressing up in black leather, thigh-high boots, and whipping a male sub silly?

My feeling is that it is often as much about looking and acting "normal" as it is about engaging in what seem to be "deviant" practices in the bedroom. Even though the average-looking person on the street cannot tell, I find that there is always something low-key and quietly self-confident about a dominant woman. This has nothing to do with looks. It is an attitude that says, "I know who I am and what I am capable of. I know what I want and how to get it. I am not so willing to bend to others' desires and choices as I once was." The confidence that comes from being in control is real once you have experienced it.

Physical domination is the control of another person by handling them, usually in a manner that assures that one person has the other in their power. In the world of consensual domination, the handling can range from gentle leading to wrestling control. At such a time, a well-fitted suit can be more useful than chains and whips. Subjecting someone to one's will can be a greater statement of control than physically overpowering them. Being a partner who knows how to make sexual decisions is as much of a statement of self-assuredness as ordering someone if you have ordered their meal.

At the most base level of physical domination is wrestling, whose object is to demonstrate that one person is physically in charge. At its heart, it becomes more about the fact of triumph than about any specific outcomes. When a wrestler finally pins their opponent to the mat, it is not the pinning that is important, it is the fact that the opponent was unable to resist. At its ideal, it subtly steers the Queen into an embrace of her power. And when strange roles are played during sexual encounters, as they often are, the Queen guides the King in his worship and surrender. She cannot lead unless she herself knows how to take orders. Success does much to boost her with the strength and independence she needs to go further in the future.

Psychological Domination

The areas of psychological domination overlap with those of physical domination. All activities of physical domination also involve psychological factors because it requires certain psychological attributes to dominate another person, just as much as it does physical attributes. Without these psychological attributes, it is impossible to properly dominate others in the real world. However, when discussing psychological domination, other matters arise which are not of relevance when discussing physical domination. Psychological domination can occur without any establishment or application of physical control. A dominant, exercising psychological control, may restrict herself to verbal communication and not touch her submissive throughout the entire period in which the submission occurs.

The establishment of psychological control requires a degree of inner strength and self-assurance. This is an area in which a dominant woman is often superior to a dominant male because her strength of character may well exceed that of a submissive, confident, submissive male. There are differences in how weaknesses and strengths influence us and determine our emotional makeup. For submissive men, strength of character, decisiveness, assertiveness, and clarity of purpose are important attributes in a dominant woman. What she is, not what she does, is the governing factor in how he feels about her, and this determines how powerful her role as a dominant is when she is presenting herself to him, addressing him, punishing him, or using him for her sexual pleasure. Dominant men rely on behavioral attributes of this kind to form their own picture of the role they should adopt when they are participating in sexual domination and to determine their own feelings of power and control during domination activities. If they regard themselves as being weak-willed, slaves, or followers in everyday life, why should they consider themselves to be otherwise in the sex game? In contrast, a dominant male can often derive much sexual pleasure from dominating a woman without having to demonstrate any dominant attributes at all.

CHAPTER 6

Practicing Safe and Consensual Female Dominance

In the popular mythic image of supremacy, it is assumed that no power other than the dominatrix's can challenge or resist a strict command. This belief is made amusingly irrelevant by the commonplace observation that dominant partners do not turn into insensate automatons. Capacity for reaction is essential for achieving the intensity of mutual erotic transport that sustains a fine scene. In practical terms, a submissive partner is safer from confusion, misunderstanding, or harm when clear, unambiguous communication flows in both directions. Here are several tips for the skillful presentation of authority.

SM scenes are mutual encounters. Conversation on the part of both people involved breathes life into them. Established mistresses and masters frequently say they have a special talent for silent communication - until they are asked how long it took to develop it. To begin with, they talk with their partners, during their explorations, throughout an encounter, and after it ends. When asked to exchange points of view about what could have transpired differently, both people in an intimate pair will learn the most if they also explain everything they were feeling. When you have finished listening to as many earnestly stated feelings as you can absorb, coax, or intimidate your partner into listening to an enlightened view of your own. This can be the start of a dialogue if neither of you drop the matter - panting, sweating, and engorged - during the course of contemplation.

The well-instructed have instinctively learned to finely orchestrate emotions, and to practice control far more often than they do the other form of active interaction, violative behavior. Attend to the small motions as well as the loud proclamations. Display high standards of your own behavior, and show that you expect high standards from your partner when enacting their own fantasies. Teach your partner by example, by teaching them about yourself, and by coaching them in the satisfying ways to express their own responses. It is okay to have to repeat yourself, even more than just once! The concept of fairness comes up at just about this point: that sex that is fair sex takes the feelings of more than one point of view into careful account.

Understanding Consent and Negotiation

A key obstacle for persons who are motivated to customarily control their sexuality but unaccustomed to directed erotic interplay lies in the art of negotiation. Particularly in historical perspectives of male sexuality, it has not been the norm to request a particular behavior in patient, comfortable, and direct language. Nevertheless, there is an organized way to arrive at a partner's acquiescence, a skill which must be newly learned—we call it negotiation. Here, a set of steps is put forth in the order in which they should be attempted—that is, the behavior is requested before it can be reinforced.

Together with trust, negotiation provides the bonding necessary to provide the context in which dominance is both most meaningful and most desired. A domination/submission pair can live without intellectual and emotional mutuality, but finding depth in the relationship may be difficult. Consensual sex acts conclude when the play ends, but honest, consensual communication continues all the days of the pair's lives.

Risk Awareness and Mitigation

We have discussed in generalities the kind of risks that accompany the dominant role. I will here detail just a few of them in more graphic form. Not because I believe that every possible sad or unfortunate event must be guarded against by strong policing or submission to authority. I do believe that people have a logical part to play in ensuring their own safety. The person who blithely walks into dense fog will be hurt, but who can reasonably prevent themselves from ever crossing a street?

Being the object of male attention - which is what I advise dominants to both cultivate and relish - can lead a woman to all sorts of ugly problems. (Say the experience other women have had to suffer with the dull glee that only jealousy allows, or else deduce it from one of the five trillion Bodice Ripper novels released yearly.) Catcalls and humiliation are the milder risks, but such things as can and do escalate quickly into violence against the girl who was aggressive enough to refuse the attention. Punches in the mouth, broken bones, stabbings, and shootings don't concern me here, either; mere plebeian suffering compared to what can happen to the minds of people who have left unshielded the kind of living energy source that female sexual appeal constitutes. All that needs to be said by way of asking you to accept that this factor could be a threat would be to remind you of all of the bat and dagger problems hackney drivers have to suffer. And nobody ever wants to see their passphrase.

CHAPTER 7

Enhancing Intimacy and Connection Through Female D

Many people find that the practice of female sexual dominance can enhance their deep emotional connection to their partner and, at the same time, help them to grow as a couple. Providing a stage for needed character transformation or becoming a catalyst for personal growth, female dominance can change the way you see your partner (for the better) every day, not just during playtime. A devoted and admiring partner who willingly wants to serve gives voice and solace to multiple intimacy concerns. What woman doesn't want to feel adored in her presence and, better still, even during her absence? Being kept on a pedestal with a submissive love partner who knows how to be attentive and available for personal expression is the ultimate intimacy boost. Even those newly engaging in the practice of consensual sexual dominance can transform these new-age play behaviors into a stunning show of long-term love and devotion to their play partners. At the end of this exploration, I will provide an exciting biblical and historical perspective on how the practice of sexual dominance can find its natural place in mainstream religion as part of the sexual development of couples in long-standing relationships.

But female sexual dominance is so much more. As you will soon see, consensual sexual dominance is an investment in growing a better partner through intimacy-building behaviors designed to improve all other manners of relationship dynamics. It isn't intimidating when we think about female sexual dominance as sex play initiation. The opportunity to arouse or be aroused, the maintenance of a slow burn of passion, and the spark of transforming monogamy into sexual ecstasy and spiritual play grant women growing perspectives of inclusivity in the shaping of sexual fulfillment. Sexual dominance is not an unexpected request because a woman's purposeful softness and influence over her environment is world-renowned. When asked, "how does a woman get things done?" it becomes clear that a woman's ability to shape her world, either through personal influence or from the comforting stability of her close-knit circle, is as important to sexual dominance as the act of taught sexual play. This demonstration of sexual dominance assuredly before play begins should emphasize her total personal awareness and personal safety in exercising the privileged invitation of playing in a man's trusted sandbox. Confidence in a personal system of safety, knowledge, and personal means to quickly end play if ever engaging in risky behavior is taken to satisfied control-seeking extremes. Only when a woman achieves mastery of safety for herself can she securely and thoroughly advance male gratification for the privilege of playing in her sandbox.

Building Trust and Vulnerability

Trust is fundamental in any relationship, but when you are playing with control and power, knowing your Domina is not going to hurt you or even break you can be essential to the experience. The two most important ways to build trust are to remember that what happens in your shadow will be said in your shadow and that your submissive's nudity is a state you must respect. The third method is that your security is the submissive's business as well. Work together to ensure your safety in your play... The deeper trust follows when you can be emotionally supportive, caring, relaxed, as well as sexually demanding and controlling - when you can be different things to each other. If it all plays out at your convenience only, the experience has a hollow ring to it, as evidently it is all about you all the time! You must also remember to protect your submissive from any danger and distress when playing with new partners. Trust both ways is essential to create the possibility for real vulnerability and thereby profound submission.

CHAPTER 8

Addressing Common Concerns and Questions

"I can't stand humiliation and torture sex play. I know you don't like them either in the way that most people imagine. They seem so outlandish and so much more violent and somewhat psychotic than most other types of SM play."

In the world of so-called "vanilla" sex, it's perfectly normal for you and your partner to not be into the same things, and perfectly okay not to do things that don't appeal or actively do feel - and are - crazy. Yet when the bondage and consensual pain is added, every person involved suddenly is expected to be into identical activities, and any sense that that's not the case is stigmatized in a way that differences over vanilla activities are not. I'm often impressed with the way I see vanilla people respect each others' idiosyncrasies, and I wish the kink world aspired to such a level of tolerance.

"So far, every femdom I have met is into humiliation. The degree of it might be different, but still it is the same thing which does not attract me. It is true that I mostly sure haven't any problems attracting a potential tops from swingers' sites, but things start to debouch at the 'what are you into' part of any chat."

Many femdoms do like play that involves humiliation. For some, a foot rub crosses the boundary of humiliation if it is given in the "servile" position. The hotness for them comes from the "woman dominates man" dynamic and less so from the particular activities involved. However, many others enjoy a wide variety of femdom activities but aren't interested in humiliation. Actually, this seems to be a common interest among new femdom players. A femdom who is new to the game and instead of straight humiliation, decides to spank her boyfriend since she already knows he likes that should be afforded the same respect and understanding as the kinkster who bounces from intelligent conversation over what the "wooden pony" might be like to experience, to discussing computer programming, to negotiating for time alone to play World of Warcraft.

Role Reversal and Gender Dynamics

This appears to be a real paradox. As dominance games are the way in which males establish who is dominant, and hierarchies help in equal sharing of resources, why are the majority of male-female interactions submissive, not dominant? Swain seems to take it a little further not only are there female CEOs of corporations, but also at home. All the women who know me, my inclinations and my situation are very supportive, and in most cases are in roles of dominance over both the boss and their male consorts. The male fellow slaves that I have met on the two occasions that I have felt able to publicly socialize as myself were complimentary and largely at a loss at why I was doing this, but there was no hostility whatsoever. On no occasion when I have been out was there hostility directed at me by anyone who knew me. I am not, however, so naive as to think that the vast majority of people have now fully accepted this role reversal. From the dressing sites and magazines where I find mutual consolidation, we all know the unpleasant realities that still stalk the world.

As a man attempting to come to terms with the way in which we are all enmeshed in the unfolding theatre of S and M that is everyday life, I sat down to write this chapter of my book 'Men in Subjection' about dominance, subjugation, and role reversal with some unease - was I seeking to put the world to rights in yet another titillating book, or was there something deeper here yet something far more tangible and less fictional to discover. I hoped so, and my journey through western history, through the centuries in which Christianity had preached love, and men had fought and struggled for preferment led me to the feeling that there was a great deal to be said for role reversal, and the exploration of the many relationships in which women correctly exercise dominance, and I tried to demonstrate this in the last section of this chapter. Since writing Men in Subjection, I have been exposed to yet more evidence for men and women leading equal and subordinate lives. The sacred rites of many women in today's church of the sexes require, sometimes hard-earned privileges over their husbands' sexual lives; get together over a drink and it is frequently the partner who will not let him express his natural dominant nature; economically there are many households that are headed by a female earning a wage packet many times larger than her husband, and these women are comfortable exercising the economic rights that derive from their dominant position over those male partners of lesser means. There are also possibly millions of people, reaching beyond any strata of class, creed, or fashion who are perfectly happy with the leader of the household being the beautifully and powerfully dominant female.

CHAPTER 9

Incorporating Play and Creativity into Female Domi

In addition to pain or discipline, dominance and submission, in its flavors of role-play, also provide opportunities for human beings to engage in play and creativity as they do in other areas of their lives, such as in jobs, little chores, amusements, interaction with family and friends, romantic relationships, religion, art, childrearing, personal grooming, travel, hobbies, and sports. Children need to play; the impulse does not fade in adulthood. We take pleasure in play and novelty. Play allows us to go from one moment of joy to the next. Creativity can cast something old into something new, something familiar to the innovative, a new mode of self-expression, whether play and creativity occur in the mind or in the world, and whether the audience is no one, oneself, one other person, or many people.

Purposefulness can make play especially thrilling; depending on its structure and circumstances, play also generates meanings other than the usual. Caked with its connotations of losing self-control and of meaning nothing, the word play is not popular. Yet we can play by playing, try out ideas, emotions, assumptions, scenarios, fantasies, and whims through the activities and ceremonies of power exchange. As with other areas of play, people may choose power exchange for its vicissitudes. Accommodating the cultures, economies, and relationships in which people live, honoring dimensions of creativity and play in the imagery and iconography of power exchange stimulates and strengthens it.

Exploring Role-Playing Scenarios

In most relationships, there is role-playing before there is red-hot sex. A well-disciplined male is eager to show off his female; a well-formed female enjoys doing so and undoubtedly will want to make sure that she has a male prepared to be proud of. Some role-playing comes naturally. For example, a male taking a female to the theater will do the necessary monkey act, unwrapping candy, offering morsels, oh, so courteously. Female dominance doesn't mean spoon-feeding a male baby food, but it does mean that the male consistently performs duties to save his female from the indignity of having to do them herself.

All of the general rules we have covered so far for the male and for the female are important, but there will be times when it is best not to emphasize them. When that knock on the door comes, the male should answer it quickly, courteously, and efficiently as instructed—quietly and without a lot of macho business. For the more explicit role-playing, where it is very clear that D&S is elephantine (we can say the bull, but not the elephant), there will be two dominant roles—the soft and the hard. Most of the time, the heterosexual male is performing the hard role, surrendering control to the soft. But any human being, and most animals, males and females both, have the capability of nurturing as well as ruling. A male subjected to the hard regimen must have time to recover—and so must a female, some, once she has gained experience, most of the time.

CHAPTER 10

The Intersection of Feminism and Female Dominance

I never wanted to be a sex guru. What interests me about sex is that it has revolutionary potential. This guide uses female sexual dominance as a lens to explore questions of power and, in particular, the intersection of personal politics and feminism. A woman who classically takes control is taking an action against social programming that would undermine that control.

Since the American women's rights movements of the late 1960s, feminism has been seen as an unequal trading card, wielded by certain women to complain that women's liberation has gone to extremely radical or unrealistic lengths. The "feminist" label is used mainly when it can be traded for something, acting as a catch-all category to preserve a certain societal view of all things gendered. If a woman is too extreme, pushy, smart, or unladylike, she is labeled feminist as a put-down. Such accusations have made many women shy away from positions where they can be criticized as stepping over the line.

Remaining a full-time professional sex worker is not an option open to many strong feminist thinkers. The psychological pressure of constantly having to perform dominance and be confident and controlling takes its toll. Personal relationships that do not live up to feminist ideals are severely limiting. In its current climate, remaining a sex worker would take away the creative edge behind this book. Depersonalization limits sex to the basest physical act. The point is not to use your sexuality as a weapon but to use your desires as power - power towards fulfilling human potential in your relationships, friendships, job, and community.

Empowerment and Agency

On the one hand, female domination is solely about control, and yet on the other, being confident and sure of yourself is an essential cornerstone of the dominance required to command such control. Sufficient confidence allows the dominatrix to totally focus on keeping her submissive in a heightened erotic state, a top priority in order to ensure that the scene will work. Part of keeping a submissive in the erotic zone so that the desired levels of control are maintained is knowing that the submissive wants to be there. This becomes more explicit as the relationship develops and irresistible force of personality, rather than force of striking physical attractiveness, becomes the central moving forces behind the couple's play.

Confidence takes practice. As with many of the skills associated with female domination, the ability to command attention and presence when required is something that many women need to learn in their professional lives and so there are many appropriate training courses available. Why not exploit that support available to you and seek to learn how to project a charismatic aura of authority? You will be doing yourself as well as your submissive partner a favor, and these are invariably the most successful relationships.

CHAPTER 11

Conclusion

Confidence in Control: An Illustrated Guide to Female Sexual Dominance illustrates various aspects of female dominance, as viewed by a sexually driven community. People of various genders have sexual dominance, and all have different approaches. This is one book from a particular perspective. People adept at playing certain roles apart from their private lives exhibit dominance. Though some of these roles may appear to go against societal expectations, people generally justify them based on their "natural" ability to perform in such roles. However, it would be simplistic to say that those who are good do so naturally and those who are bad do so unnaturally. This book covers both good and bad scenarios.

This book aims to encourage those who would like to adopt the subject position described. It contains a variety of poses and scenario descriptions that show a female in control. Some photos may not match the top of the pose to the bottom or the explanation for the scene to real life. Experienced individuals know that what you see on the cover, or any other illustration, shows only one moment and perspective of the dominant. Experienced community members know that things can change and that they need to be flexible because communities have different expectations, desires, and dilemmas. To those whose body shape does not resemble those in this book, embody the attitude of control. Know that the sophisticated look on a dominant face, the clothes, and the background show you that it is not the shape or size of the individual that counts; it is the ability to exercise control. Confidence rules. Period.

Key Takeaways and Reflections

As we near the end of our journey, I would like to share a few final thoughts as well as remind you how special and important you are. We have just traveled through the pages of practical tools, insightful information, though provoking ideas, and reflections on sexual dominance and, most importantly, you made it through. If you have been taking your time and only trying some of the exercises, that's fine, too. Share them with your partner for talking, playing, or experimenting. Overall, I encourage you to do what's comfortable for you. If inspired, share the book with a friend, group, or sex education class.

I hope you have found some guidance as you carve out your path as the fierce, beautiful, and confident sexual being you are. Most importantly, remember there is something I hope you take to heart and keep in the forefront of your being. You are fine just the way you are. By possessing a sexual essence that is strong and confident, yet tender and caring, you embrace a natural, free flowing positive energy. That's a level of success far beyond any accomplishment that is your guide and will enhance every phase of your life. It is one that makes you an awesome human being as well as an incredible sexual partner.